MW01537818

This notebook belongs to

Email

Signature Planner Journals

www.signatureplannerjournals.com
www.signatureplannerjournals.co.uk

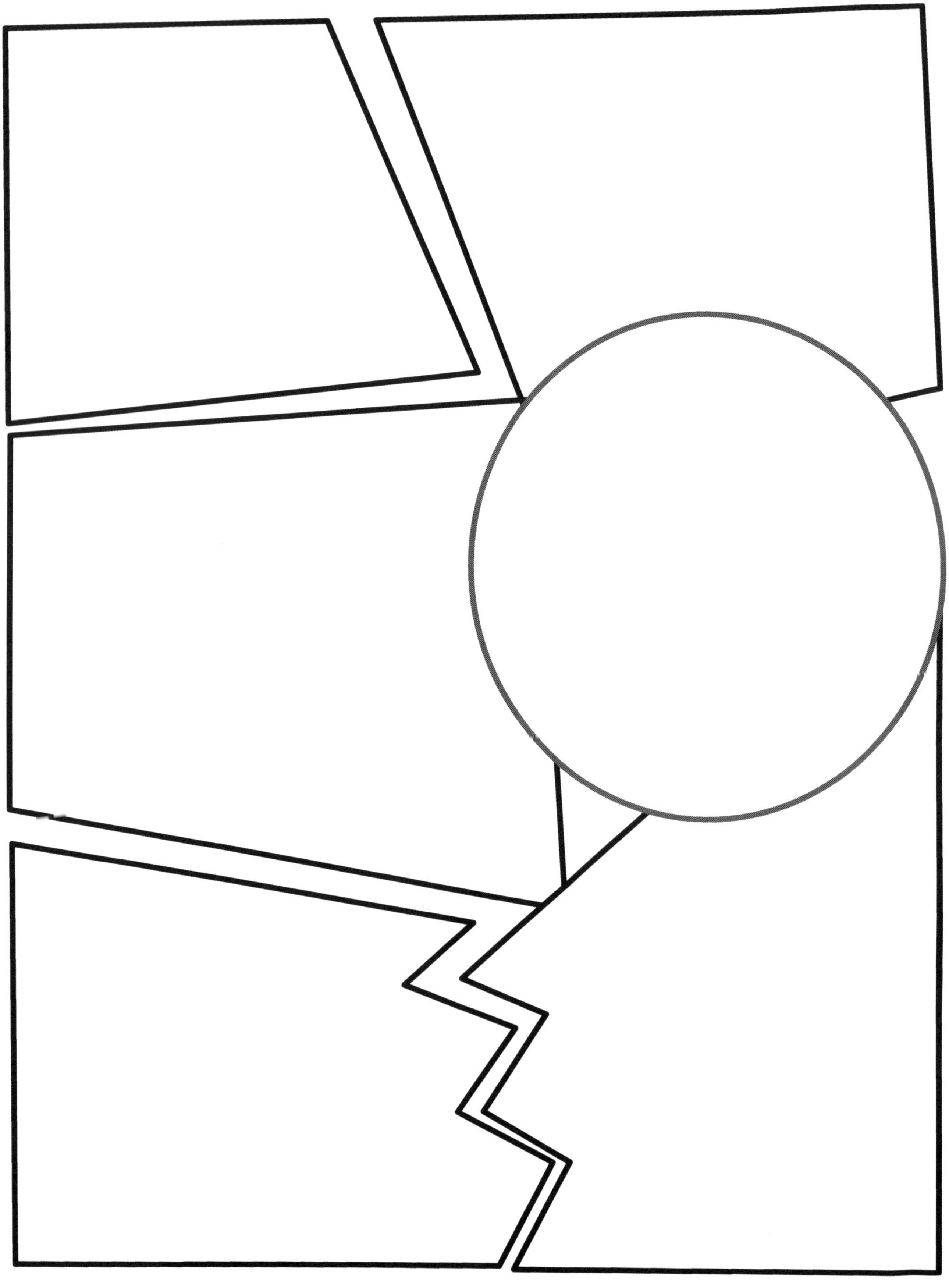

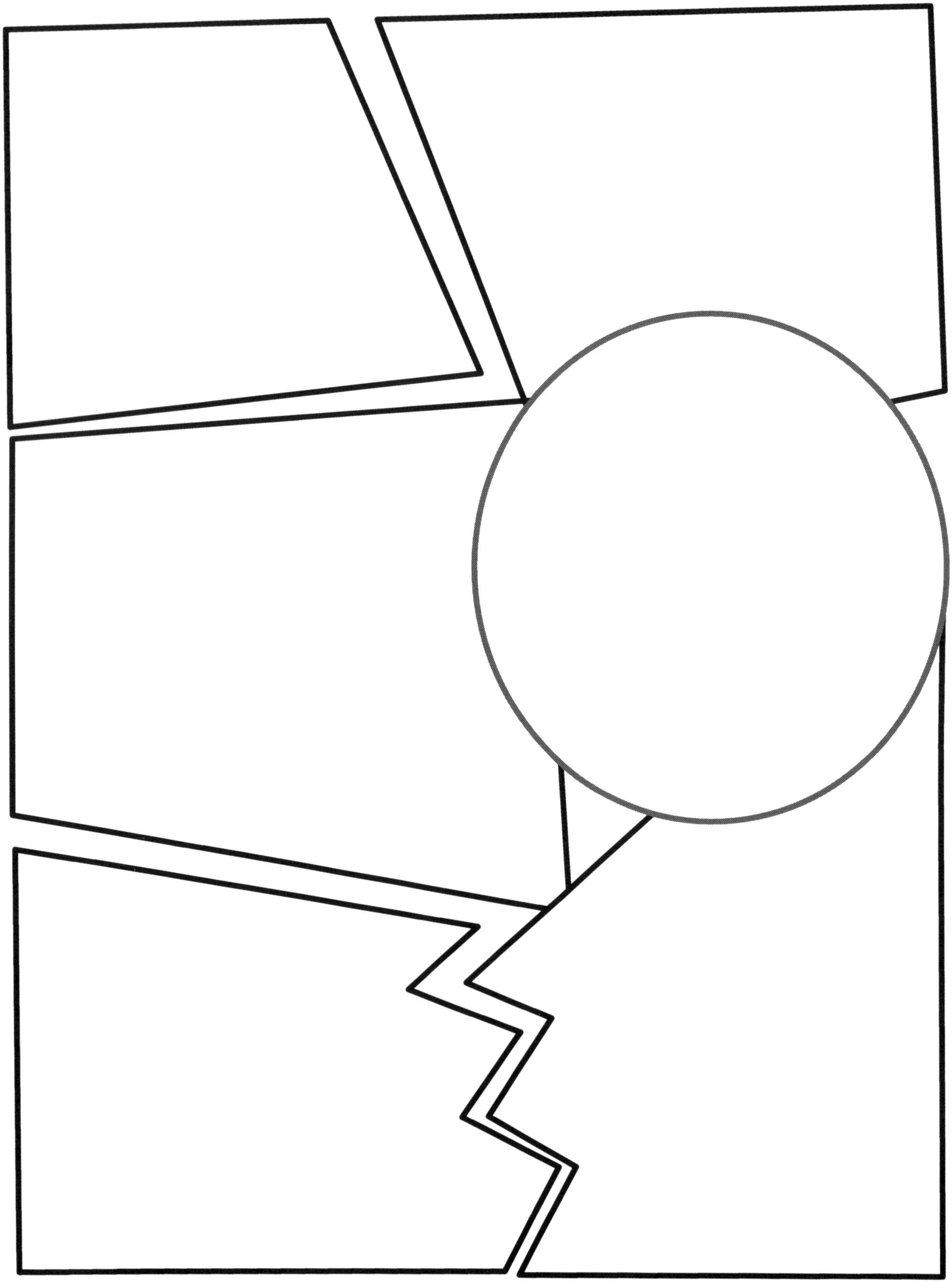

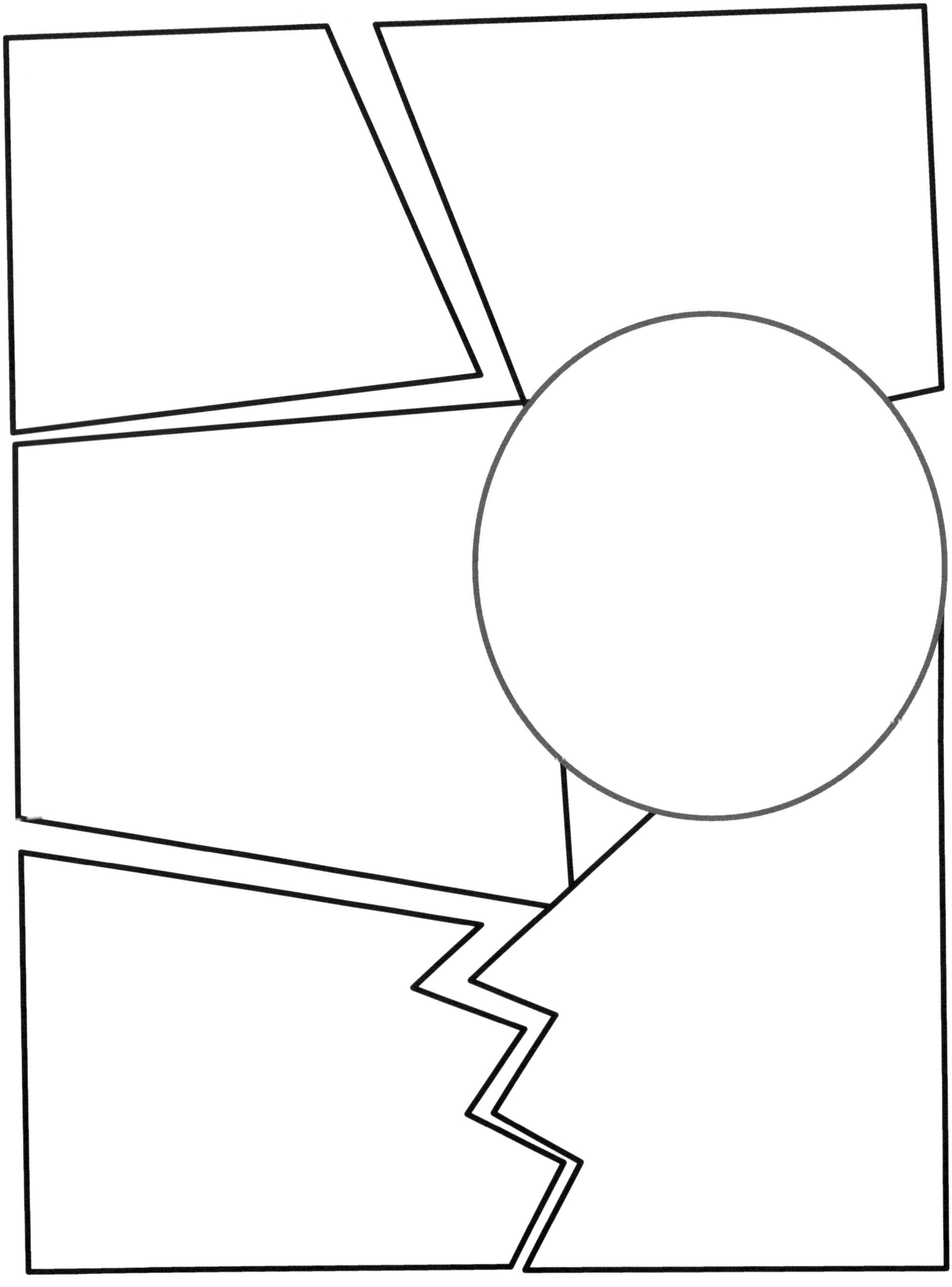

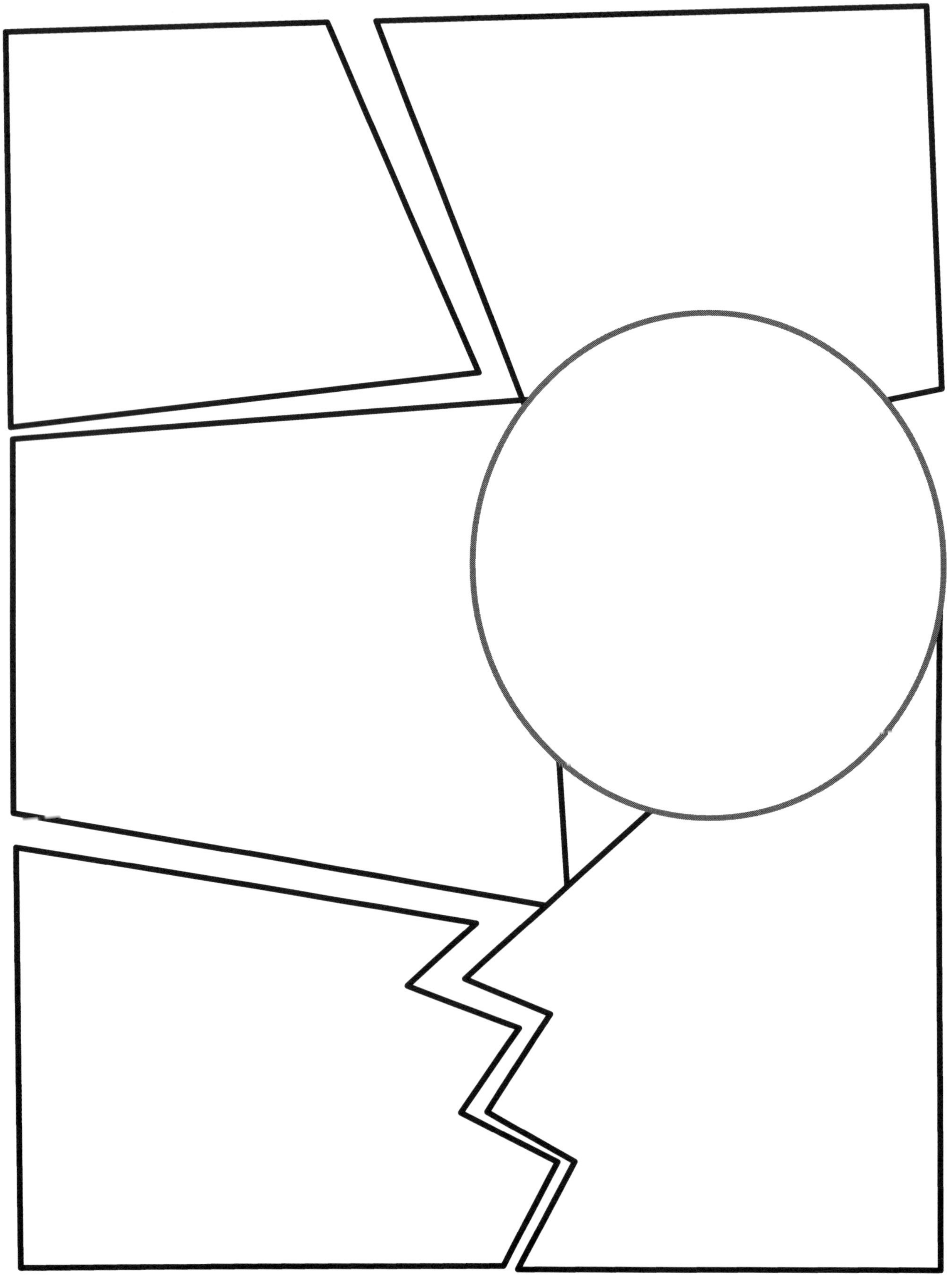

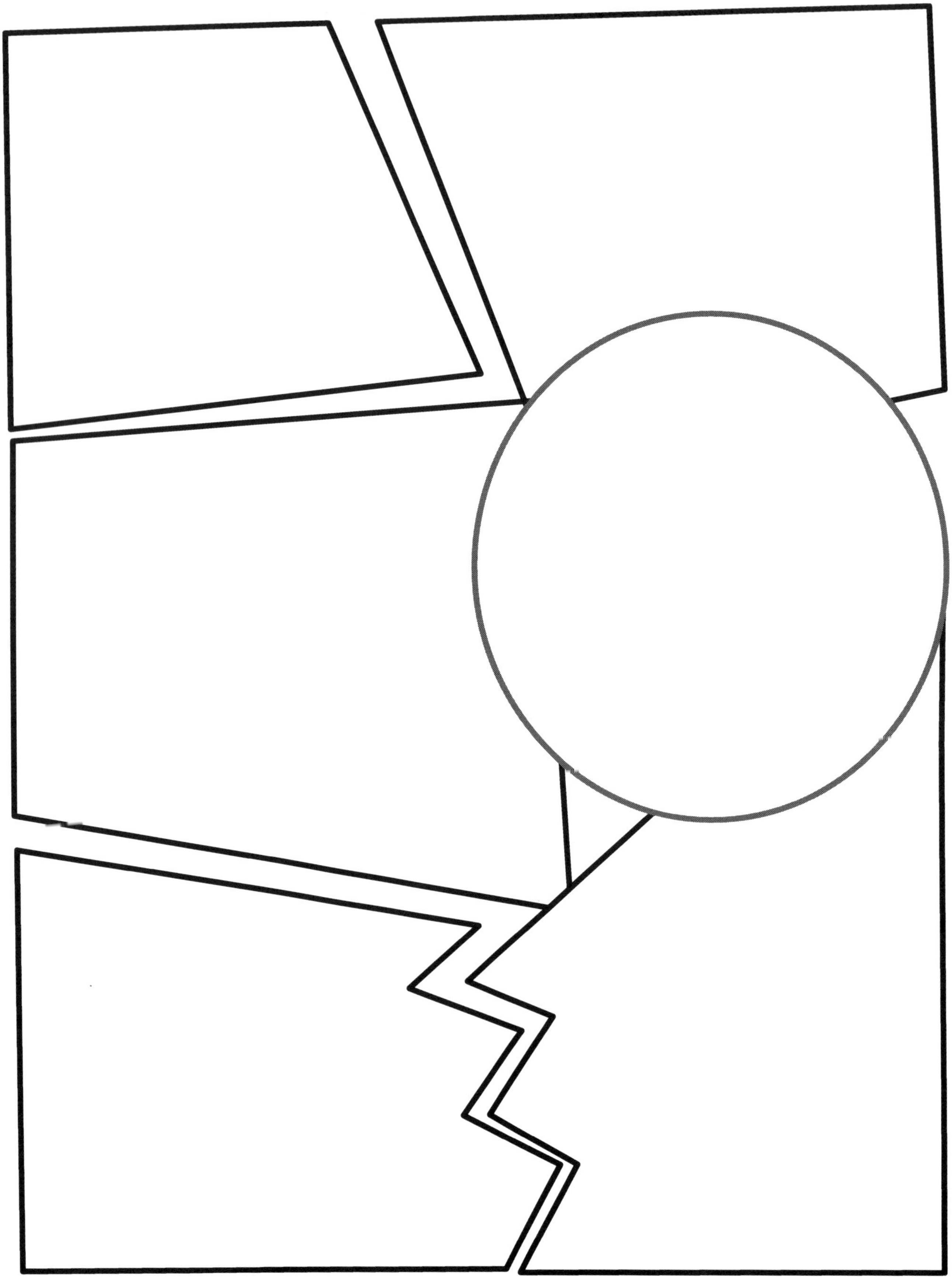

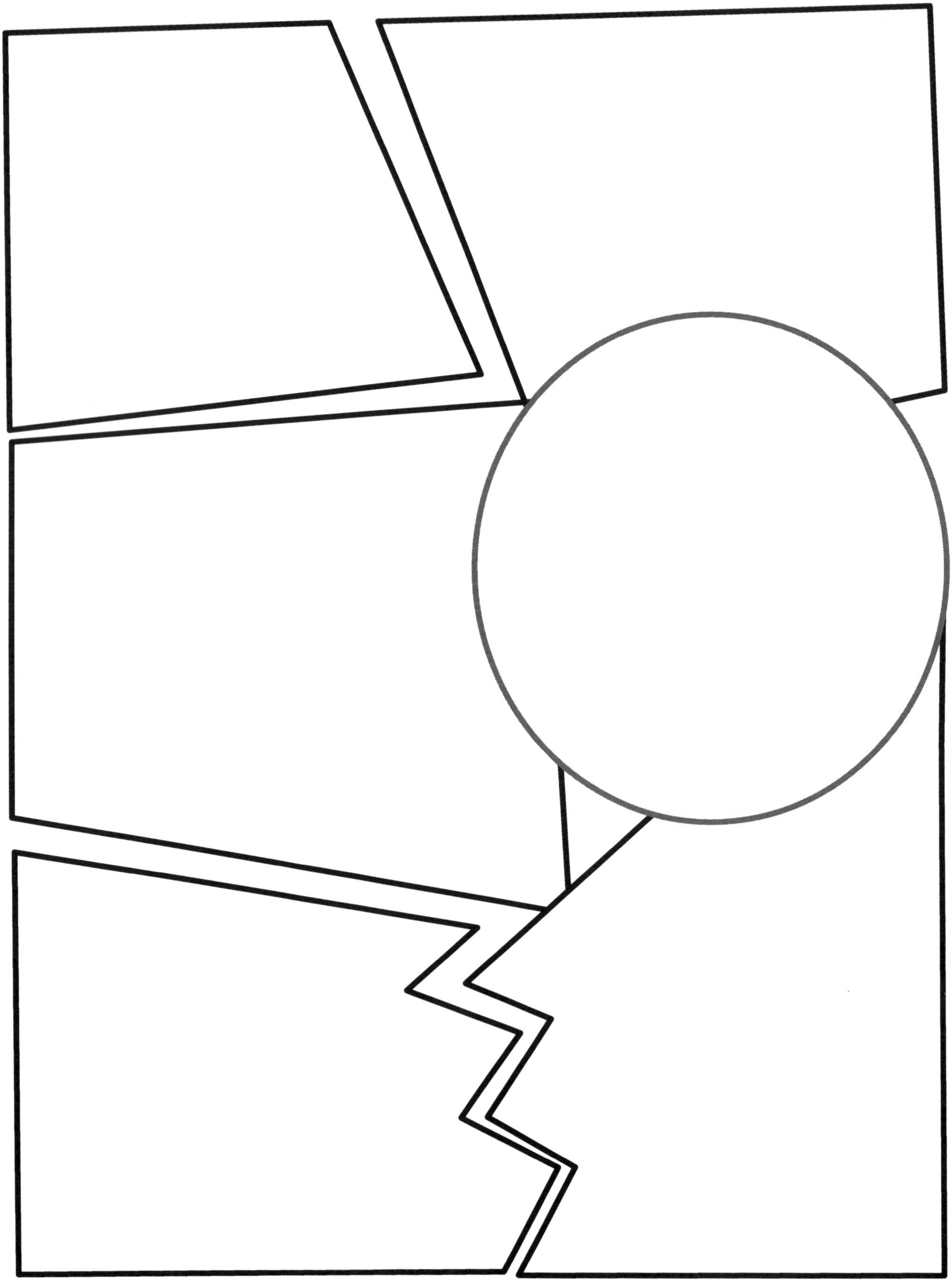

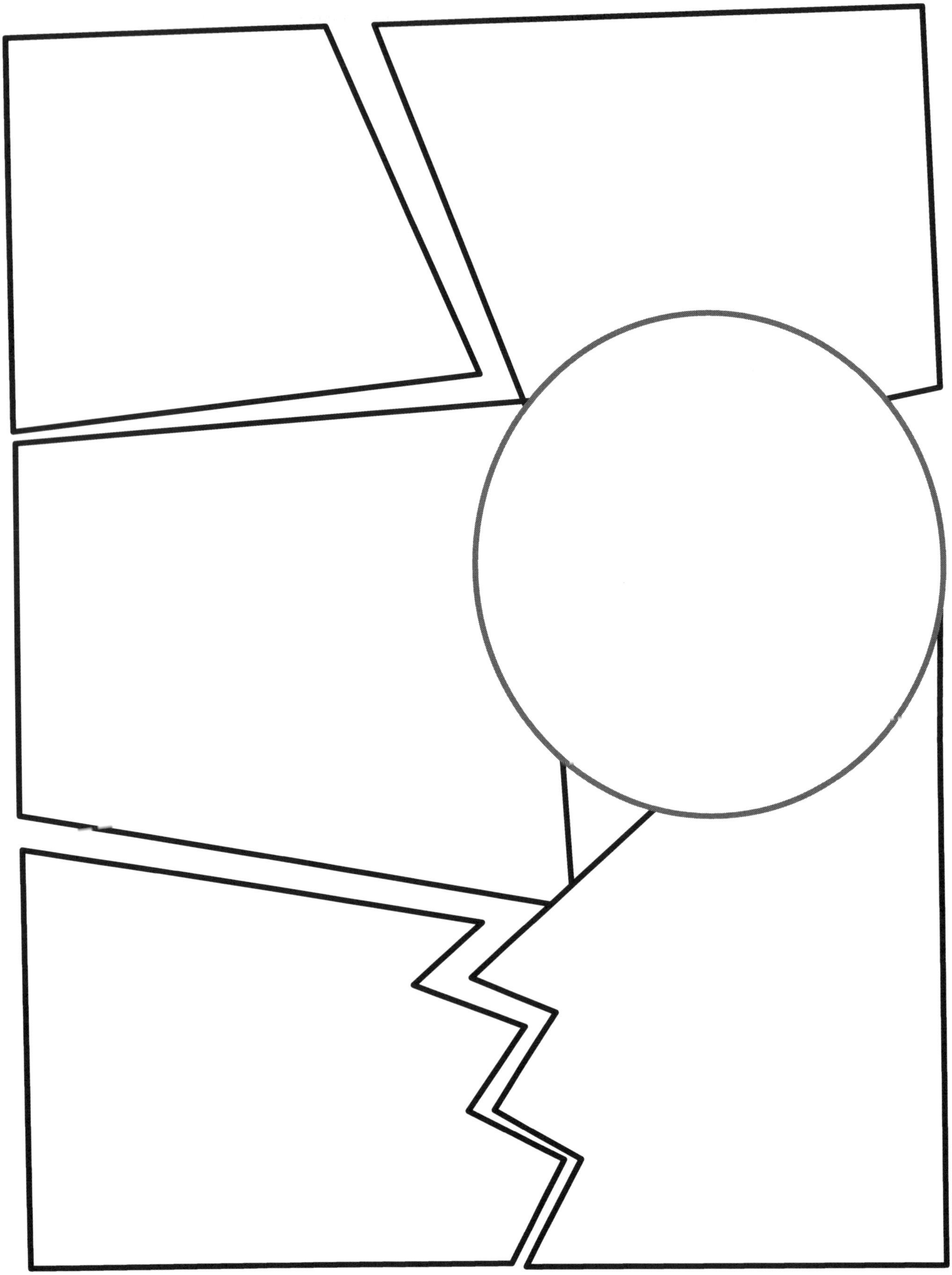

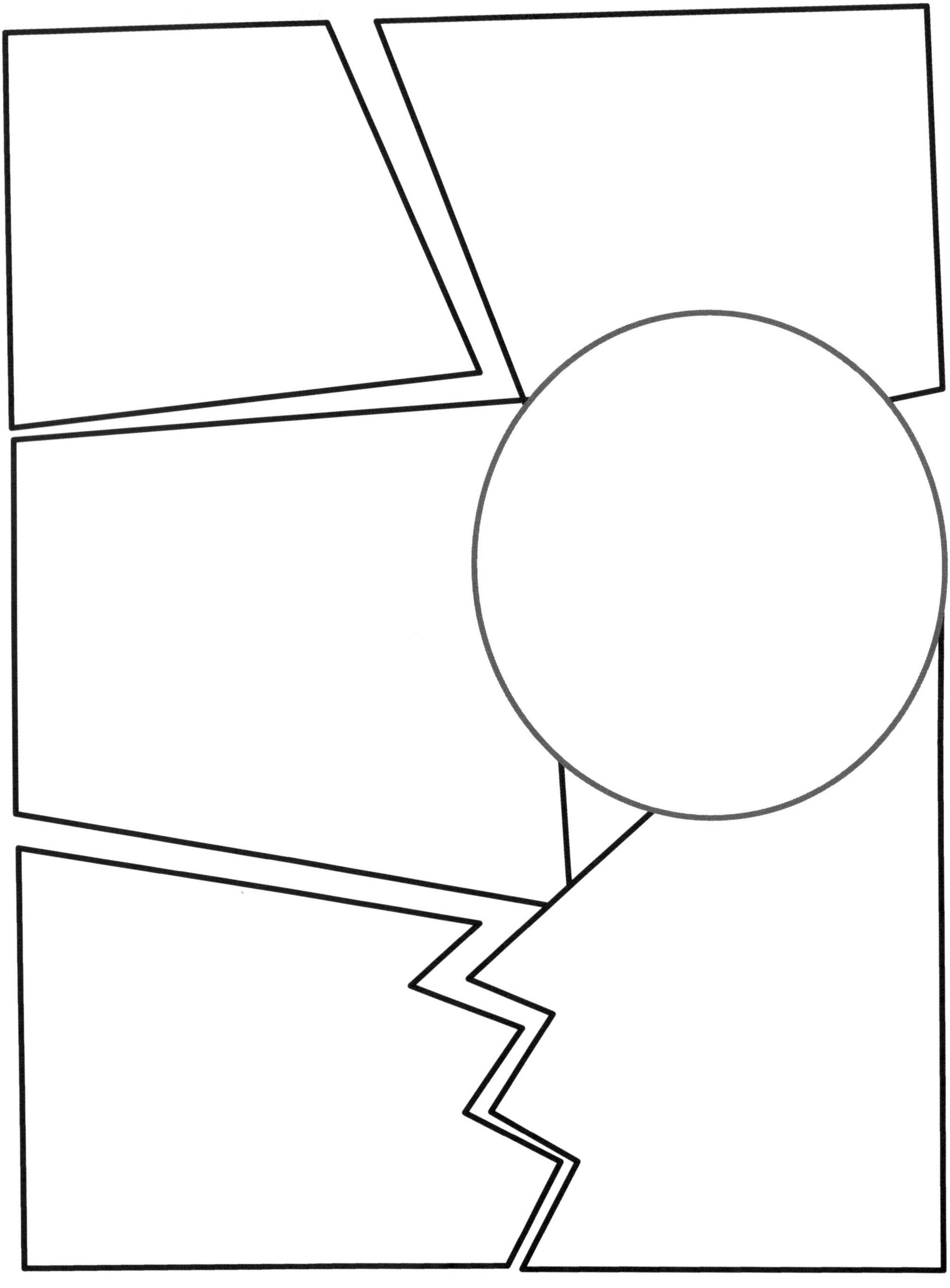

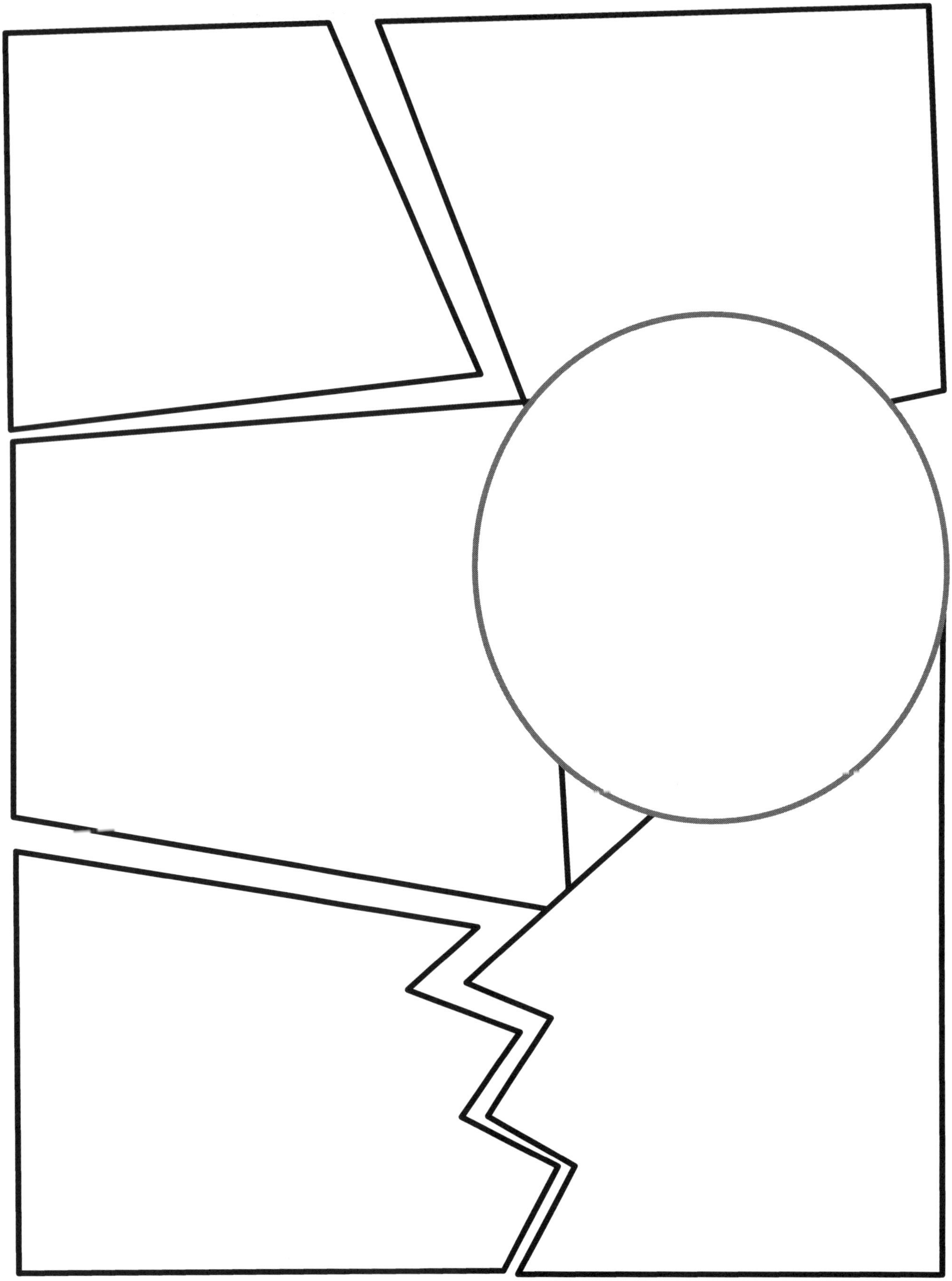

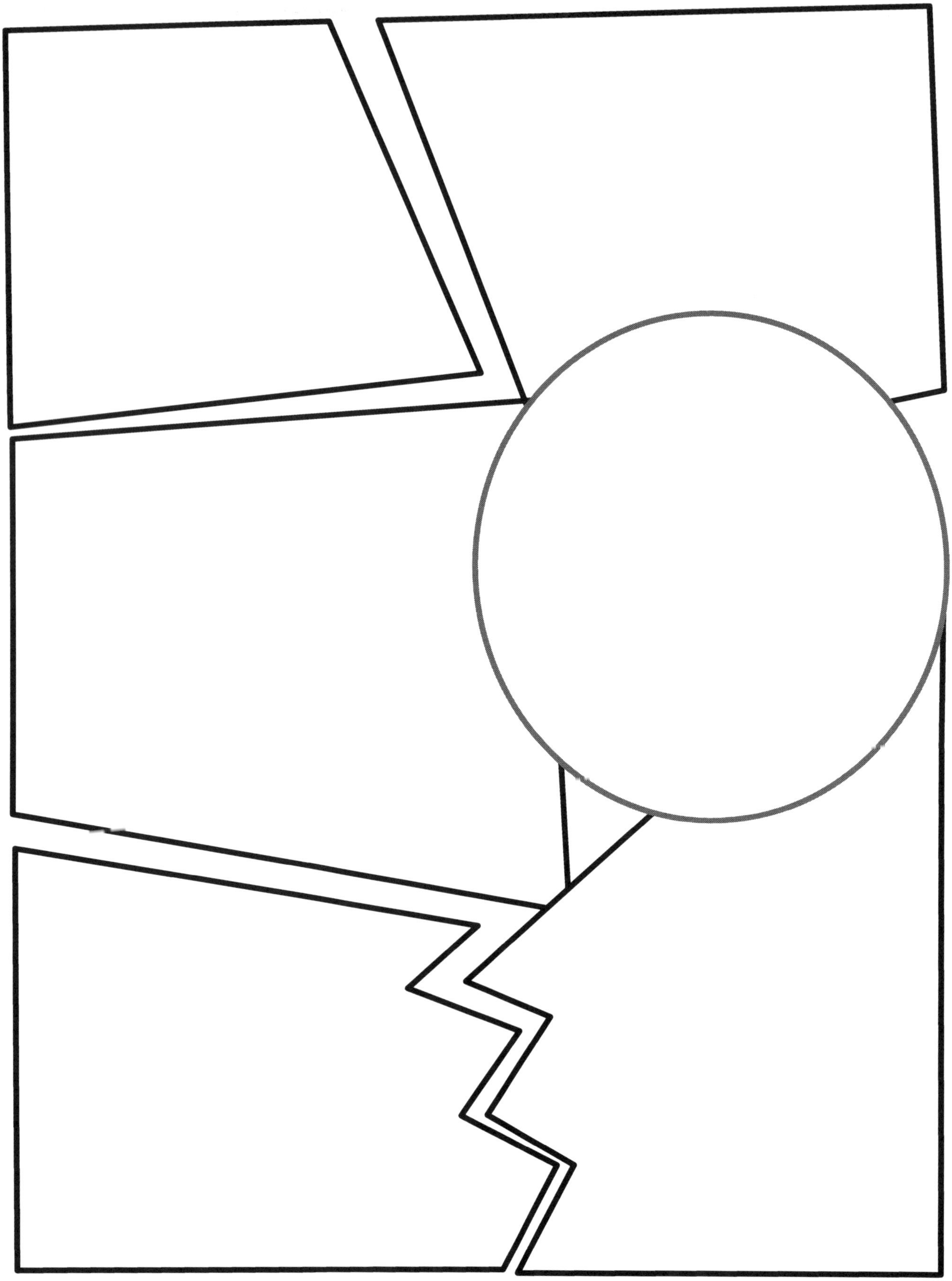

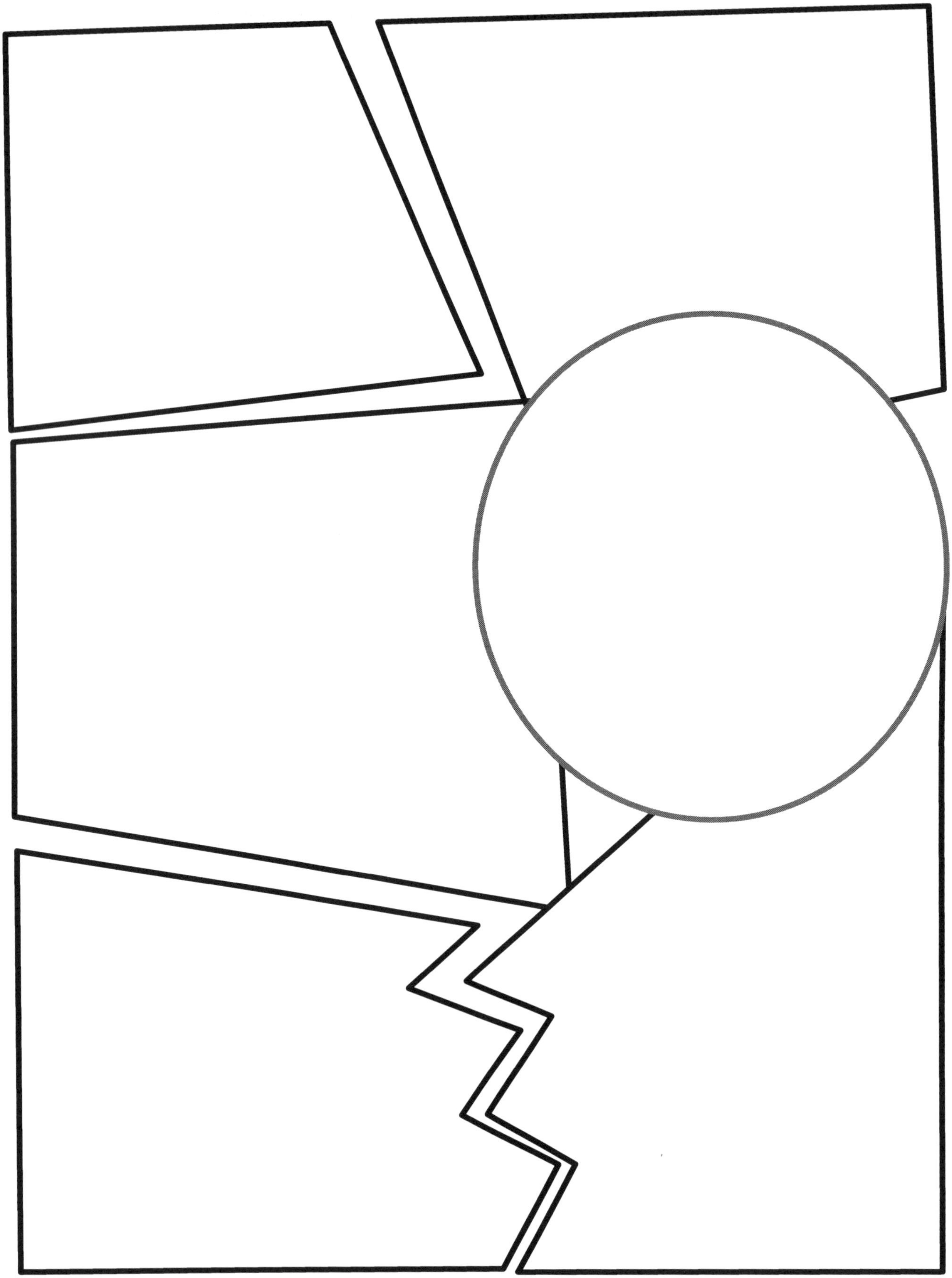

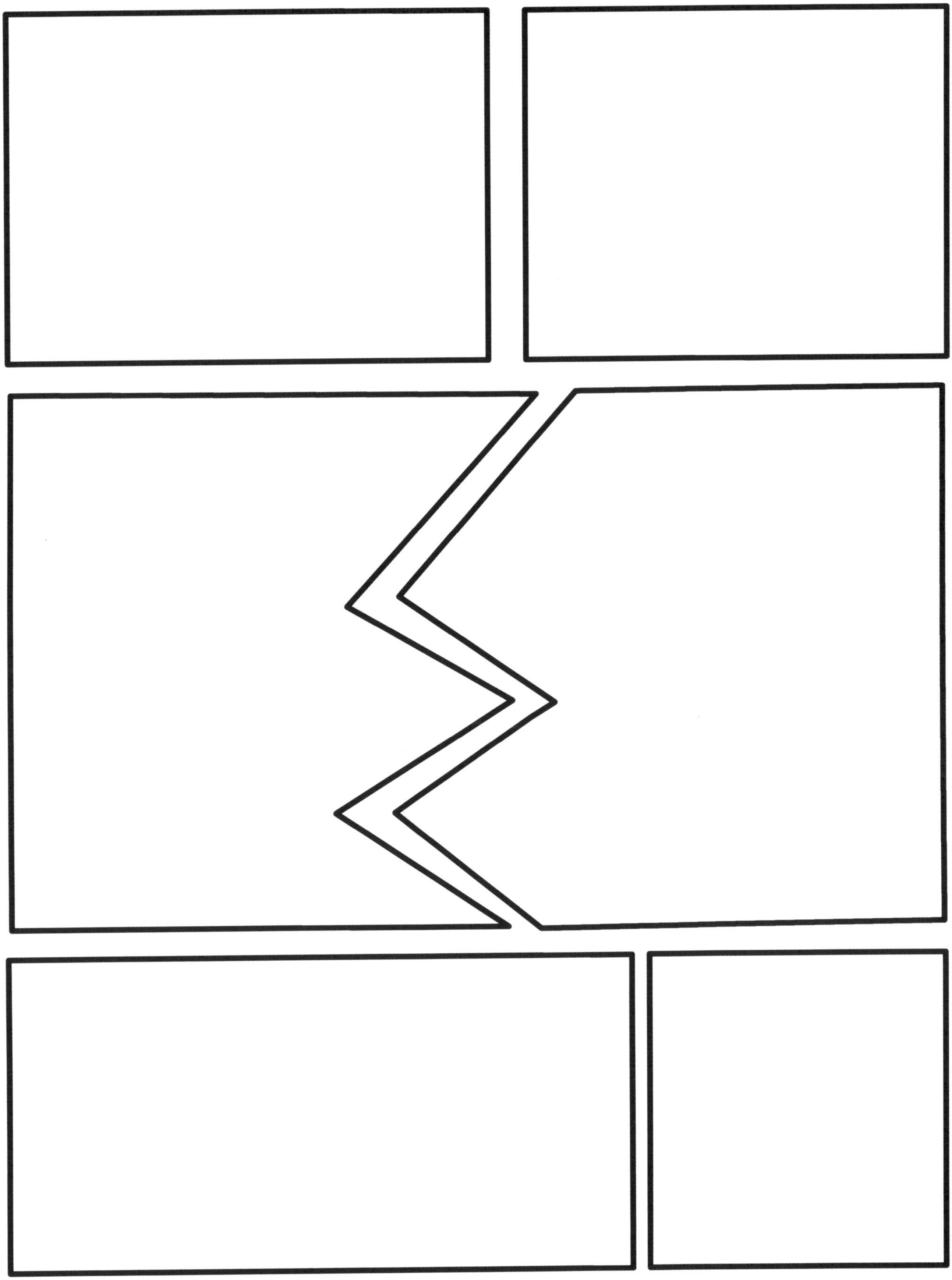

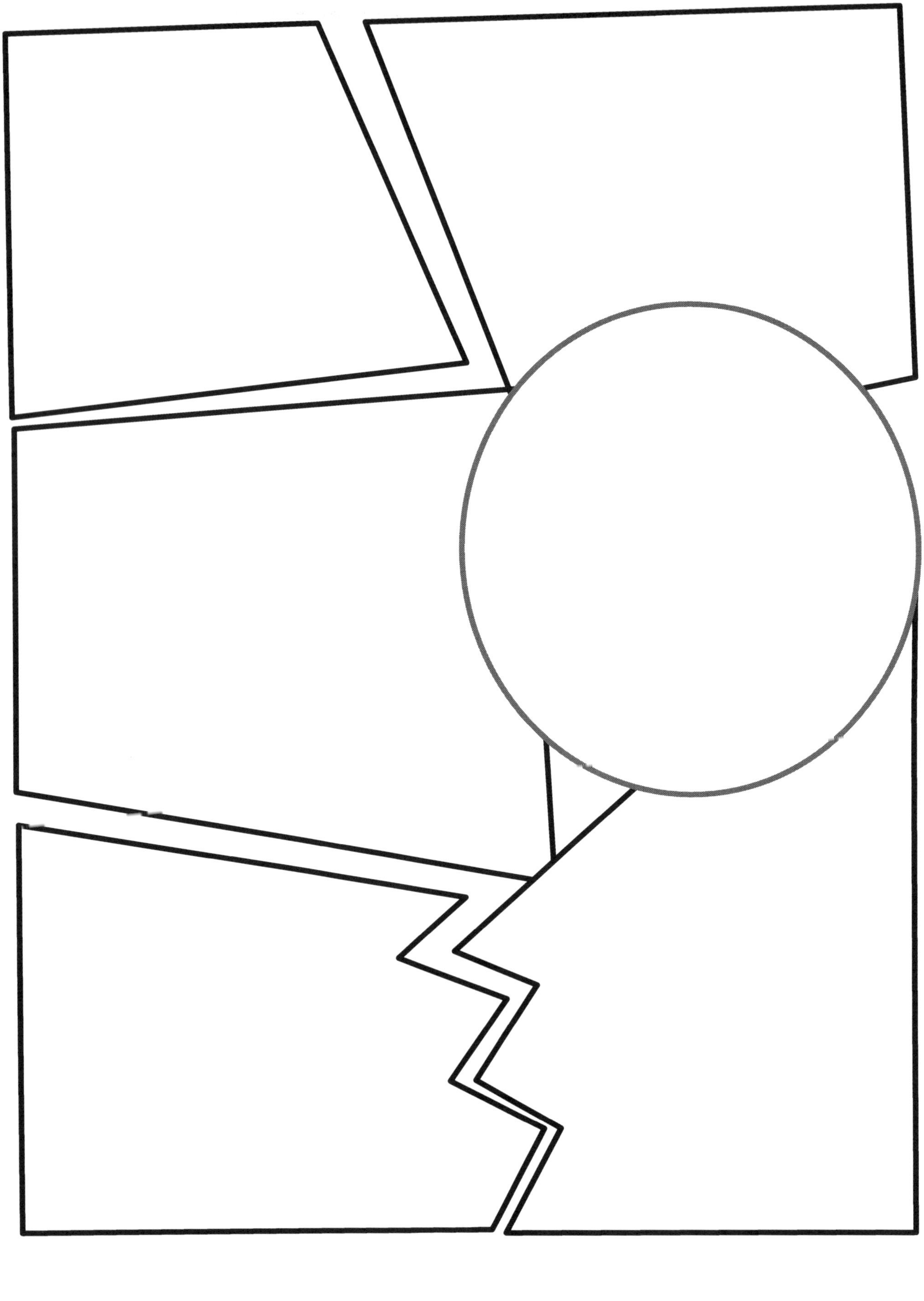

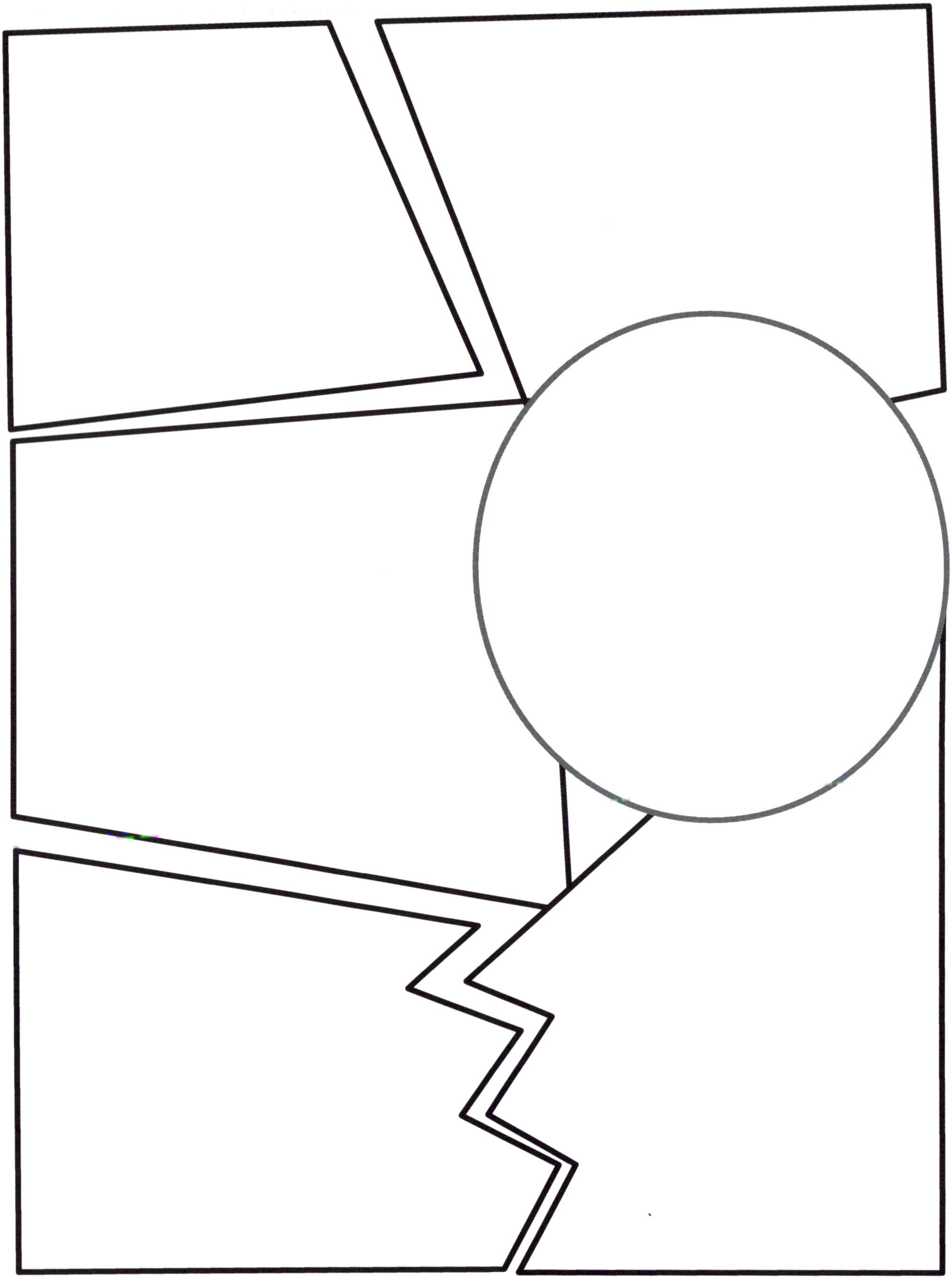

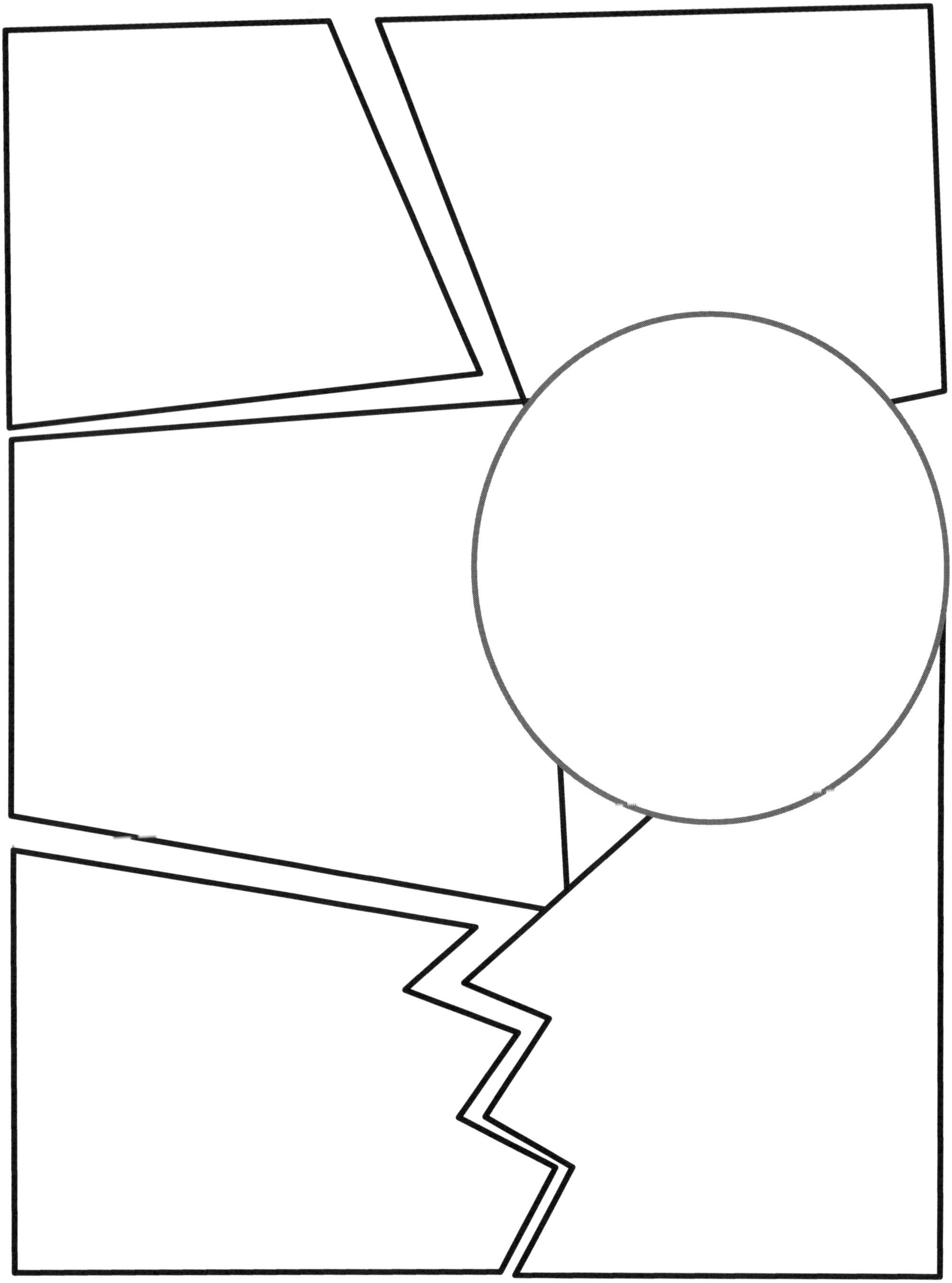

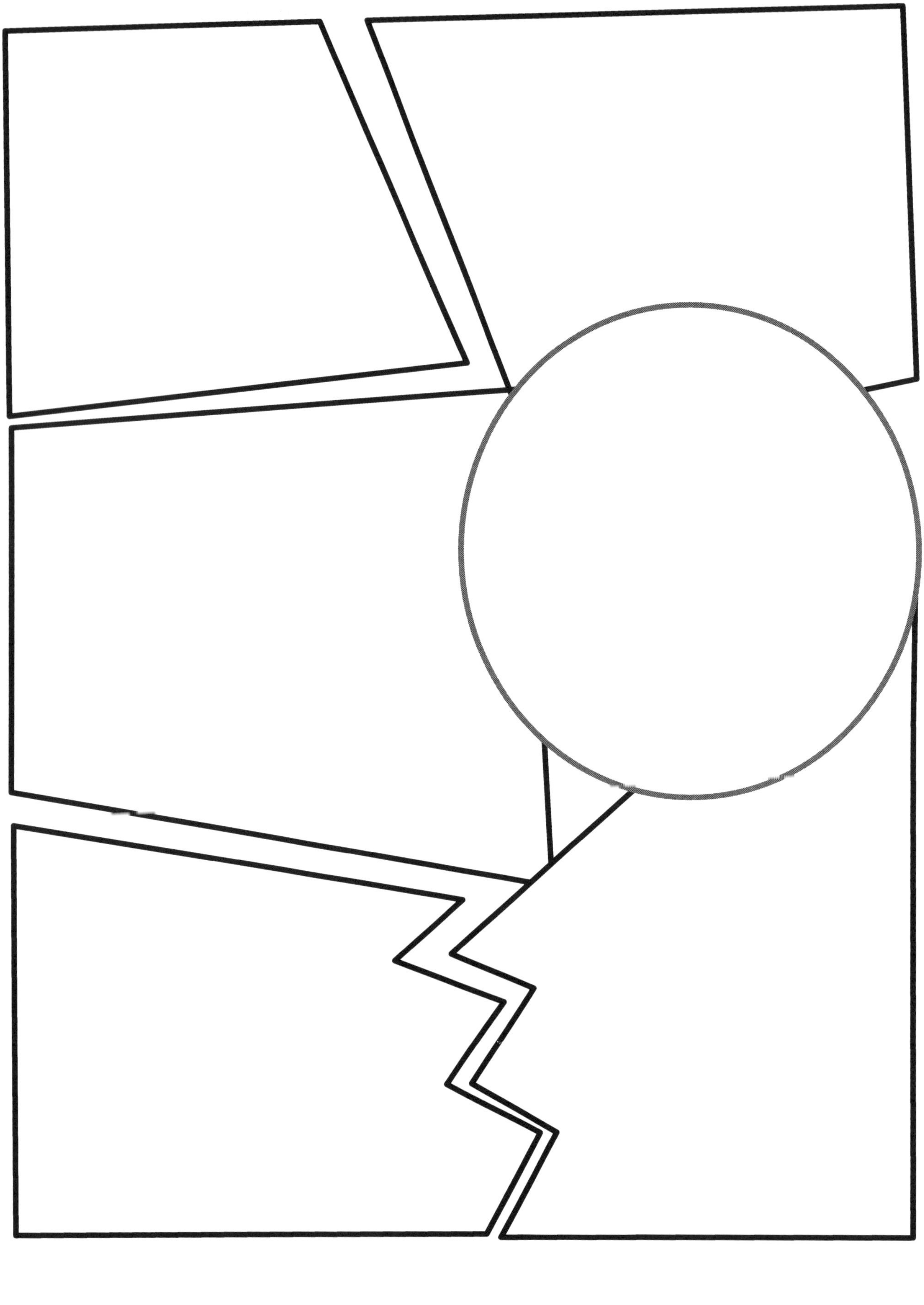

Made in the USA
Las Vegas, NV
22 December 2021

39200297R10063